A Pamphlet of Love

A Beginner's Walk

Author
Angela Jefferson

Illustrations
Wangui Munyua & Angela Jefferson

Welcome to the Kingdom of God

Choosing Light

For God so loved the world, that he gave his only Son,
that whoever believes in him should not perish but have eternal life.
John 3:16 ESV

Welcome to Your BEST LIFE!

Psalms 34:8 NKJV
Oh, taste and see that the LORD is good; Blessed is the man who trusts in Him!

Jeremiah 29:11 NKJV
For I know the thoughts that I think toward you, says the LORD, thoughts of peace and not of evil, to give you a future and a hope.

This is the best decision you can make. Deciding to learn and grow in all things of the Lord.

The Lord asked me to write a pamphlet of love highlighting the things good and bad that I went through seeking Him. He said they will need it. And the writing journey began.

What I share in this pamphlet is what I experienced as I started going to church, reading the Bible, and spending time with the Lord.. The revelations and downloads from My Father in heaven were healing and transforming. May He speak to you as you read. I am convinced that His purpose for this pamphlet will be done.

At the beginning of my true walk with the Lord, I remember a beautiful jaw-dropping moment. I had just woken up and was just lying around. I heard the Lord say to me, I love you. I said, I know because You love the world. The Lord said to me again, I love you. I said I know because you love the whole world. Then He said I love YOU and it hit me. All of a sudden I felt His overwhelming love. I just started crying uncontrollably. I felt like I was lifted and spinning around with His beautiful light on me. I will never forget that precious moment when I realized I was truly loved by God, and not by default. He loves ME.

He loves you so much. Pursue Him as He Pursues you. Your life will be forever changed for your good

Congratulations!

As you follow Jesus you are following Truth

The masquerade is over/ The Truth stands and the lies . dies over your life. The Lord will show you who you really are

This is the unveiling of deception

It is about you in growing and learning

But it is not <u>All</u> about you

It is the uniting and empowering the Body of Christ to do God's will

Rejoice!

You get to receive God's love that surpasses all understanding

You get to know God on a personal level

You get to live a life filled with power and strength through our Lord and Savior Jesus Christ

You get to work with The Kingdom Of God for the betterment of mankind

You get to be raised from death to a love-filled life with great purpose and meaning

THIS IS YOUR TRANSFORMATION!

Own it, Receive it fully & Be glad in it!

Your personal relationship with The Father, The Son, & The Holy Spirit
You will come to realize the power of His love for you

Trust God and Trust His Love Process
When change happen there is a processing that occurs

Choose to Live in the Goodness of GOD
Stay in the positive and KNOW that God has you. Choose to Believe what He says about you

There Is No Greater Love

No one can love you the way God does

Romans 5:8 NKJV
8 But God demonstrates His own love toward us, in that while we were still sinners, Christ died for us.

Intimacy

Growing an intimate relationship with God, Jesus and Holy Spirit will now define who you are and whom you are becoming.

There will be moments of struggle because there is a new awareness of self that you may not like. Look at it and go through the process of healing. Do not resist the change; allow this discomfort to move you to the next level. Always be open to hear what the Lord is saying or showing you through the processing.

Sometimes we tend to shut out what doesn't feel good. Keep our eyes on God, He will walk with us through it all

Kingdom Terms

Trust - firm belief in the reliability, truth, ability, and strength of God.

The Kingdom of God - also refers to as the Kingdom of Heaven - is the spiritual realm over which God reigns as king or the fulfillment on Earth of God's will.

Acknowledge- accept or admit the existence or truth of God

Kingdom Terms

Seek - attempt to find

Obedient - complying or willing to comply with orders or requests; submissive to God's will.

Insight - the capacity to gain an accurate and deep intuitive understanding of God's will

Covenant- an agreement with God

Kingdom Mindset

Our desire is for the Heart & Mind of Christ.

COMMITMENT
I want to be ONE with the Lord. I want to have a true understanding and a true love for Him. I want to have a relationship with Him and know Him intimately. This is the ultimate goal to know God for myself. Is this what you want? A change in mindset is necessary, embrace it.

Romans 12:1-2 AMP

12 Therefore I urge you, brothers and sisters, by the mercies of God, to present your bodies [dedicating all of them yourselves, set apart] as a living sacrifice, holy and well-pleasing to God, which is your rational (logical, intelligent) act of worship. 2 And do not be conformed to this world [any longer with its superficial values and customs], but be transformed and progressively changed [as you mature spiritually] by the renewing of your mind [focusing on godly values and ethical attitudes], so that you may prove [for yourselves] what the will of God is, that which is good and acceptable and perfect [in His plan and purpose for you].
(The Amplified Bible)

Kingdom Life

Citizens Get to Live in Love

No Fear 2 Timothy 1:7
7 For God has not given us a spirit of fear, but of power and of love and of a sound mind.

No Condemnation Romans 8:1
8 There is therefore now no condemnation to those who are in Christ Jesus, who do not walk according to the flesh, but according to the Spirit.

Unity with the Body of Christ 1 Cor.1:10
10 Now I plead with you, brethren, by the name of our Lord Jesus Christ, that you all speak the same thing, and that there be no divisions among you, but that you be perfectly joined together in the same mind and in the same judgment.

Perfect Love 1 John 4:18
18 There is no fear in love, but perfect love casts out fear because fear involves torment. But he who fears has not been made perfect in love.

Kingdom Life

In Power **Philippians 4:13**
13 I can do all things through Christ who **strengthens** me.

In Freedom **Galatians 5:1**
1 Stand fast therefore in the liberty by which Christ has made us free, and do not be entangled again with a yoke of bondage.

In Joy **Psalm 16:11**
11 You will show me the path of life; In Your presence *is* fullness of joy; At Your right hand *are* pleasures forevermore.

In Peace **Philippians 4:6-7**
6 Be anxious for nothing, but in everything by prayer and supplication, with thanksgiving, let your requests be made known to God; 7 and the peace of God, which surpasses all understanding, will guard your hearts and minds through Christ Jesus.

Kingdom Life

Resting In God

In Mercy **1 Peter 1:3**

3 Blessed be the God and Father of our Lord Jesus Christ, who according to His abundant mercy has begotten us again to a living hope through the resurrection of Jesus Christ from the dead.

In Grace **Ephesians 2:8-9**

8 For by grace you have been saved through faith, and that not of yourselves; it is the gift of God, 9 not of works, lest anyone should boast.

In No Fear and Perfect Love **Deut 31:6**

Be strong and of good courage, do not fear nor be afraid of them; for the Lord your God, He is the One who goes with you. He will not leave you nor forsake you."

Kingdom Steps

God is there for every step of the way

Joshua 1:9 New International Version (NIV)
9 Have I not commanded you? Be strong and courageous. Do not be afraid; do not be discouraged, for the Lord your God will be with you wherever you go."

Be Confident in God's love for you. He loves you so much and He wants you to know it. His thoughts of you are not as your thoughts of yourself. Allow Him to show who you are through His eyes. He desire you and want to give you all that He has set aside just for you

Kingdom Steps

- **The Bible Enrich your knowledge of God's Word**
  Get to know God through His Word, the Bible. Just start and the Lord will do the rest.

- **God shines a light on your path.**
  He will guide you and do the work in you if you surrender and allow Him to.

- **Surround yourself with Believers of Christ**
  Get around like minded people. Find a church in person or online.

- **Pray Praise and Worship**
  There is no wrong way. Do not be concern of how others do it. You will have your own way to speak to the Lord. Just do it even if it feels weird, Press on You will be amazed!

Kingdom Steps

- Trust God through it all.

- Allow God's love to embrace you fully.

- Have Faith regardless of how it look like or feel like

- Be persistent and push through the yucky stuff.

- Be HONEST about what is revealed about yourself.

- Continue to dig deeper when you want to turn away.

- Spiritual gifts will begin to grow, do not resist instead pursue them.

Deuteronomy 31: (NIV)
6 Be strong and courageous. Do not be afraid or terrified because of them, for the Lord your God goes with you; he will never leave you nor forsake you."

A little insight

My Experience

- I was afraid of the unknown & didn't know what to expect
- I was confused and was apprehensive about asking questions in fear of being judged
- When I started going to church felt uncomfortable, unworthy, and not enough because I was new
- The Push Back is Real - Many of my family and friends did not understand what was happening with me and and they did not like it.
- I was worried about what others think of me.
- I had to get out of my own way
- Believe God's word and have Faith that the Lord has only good intentions for me
- Things are revealed in levels - cleaning me out as I go through God's forever love process
- Realizing and embracing God's love for Me -was a game-changer. Feeling the Love of God, It is not like no other. I was forever changed
- These things were revealed to me about myself as I went through the process. It is not always easy but definitely worth it. I lived in fear and condemnation until I surrendered myself to the Lord and He did the rest

My Experience

I received a word from the Holy Spirit one day, "You think it's going to be easy because it's God? I quickly agreed with "Yes!" And He said, "It will not always be easy, But I am with you and will hold you up."

It is going to get difficult sometimes but God says, "Fear not I am with you."
We have to trust and believe what the Lord says about us and what He says to us. The intimacy will grow as you learn more about him.

The scriptures that I am sharing in the next pages have kept me in the right mindset as I began my walk. They are still a constant help to me. I know they will help you as well. As you grow, the Holy Spirit will highlight scripture for your walk with Him. He is faithful.
I call them your "go to" scriptures.

Scriptures

John 3:16 KJV 16 For God so loved the world, that he gave his only begotten Son, that whosoever believeth in him should not perish, but have everlasting life.

Proverbs 3:5-6 NIV 5 Trust in the Lord with all your heart and lean not on your own understanding; 6 in all your ways submit to him and he will make your paths straight.

2 Timothy 1:7 NKJV 7 For God has not given us a spirit of fear, but of power and of love and of a sound mind.

Romans 10:9-10 NKJV 9 that if you confess with your mouth the Lord Jesus and believe in your heart that God has raised Him from the dead, you will be saved. 10For with the heart one believes unto righteousness, and with the mouth, confession is made unto salvation.

And More Scriptures

Romans 8:31-32 NKJV 31 What then shall we say to these things? If God is for us, who can be against us? 32He who did not spare His own Son, but delivered Him up for us all, how shall He not with Him also freely give us all things?

Isaiah 55:8-9 NKJV 8 For My thoughts are not your thoughts, Nor are your ways My ways, says the Lord. 9 For as the heavens are higher than the earth, So are My ways higher than your ways, And My thoughts than your thoughts.

2 John 1:3 NIV 3 Grace, mercy and peace from God the Father and from Jesus Christ, the Father's Son, will be with us in truth and love.

Isaiah 54:17 NKJV 17 No weapon formed against you shall prosper, And every tongue which rises against you in judgment You shall condemn. This is the heritage of the servants of the Lord, And their righteousness is from Me," Says the Lord.

Galatians 1:10 ESV 10 For am I now seeking the approval of man, or of God? Or am I trying to please man? If I were still trying to please man, I would not be a servant of Christ.

IN CHRIST I AM

I AM VICTORIOUS
1 Corinthians 15:57 says:
57. But thanks be to God, who gives us the victory through our Lord Jesus Christ. (NKJV)

I AM BEAUTIFUL
Song of Solomon 4:7 says:
7. You are altogether beautiful, my love; there is no flaw in you. (ESV)

I AM GOD'S
Isaiah 43:1 says:
1. But now, thus says the LORD, who created you, O Jacob, And He who formed you, O Israel: "Fear not, for I have redeemed you; I have called you by your name; You are Mine. (NKJV)

I AM REDEEMED
Ephesians 1:7 says:
7. In Him we have redemption through His blood, the forgiveness of sins, according to the riches of His grace. (NKJV)

I AM A NEW CREATION
2 Corinthians 5:17 says:
17. Therefore, if anyone is in Christ, he is a new creation; old things have passed away; behold, all things have become new. (NKJV)

I AM MORE THAN A CONQUEROR
Romans 8:37 says:
17. Yet in all these things we are more than conquerors through Him who loved us. (NKJV)

SEEK YOUR TRUE IDENTITY IN CHRIST

Salvation Prayer

If you have not given your life over to Christ
I would love to give you the opportunity to do so now
Please say out loud

A Sincere Cry

Thank you Jesus for your sacrifice. I believe you died on the cross and rose on the third day for my sins. Come into my life as my Lord and Savior. Help me walk the path that you have so lovingly put before me. I desire to be with you always

(Romans 10:9-10, NIV)

If you declare with your mouth, "Jesus is Lord," and believe in your heart that God raised him from the dead, you will be saved. For it is with your heart that you believe and are justified, and it is with your mouth that you profess your faith and are saved.

Next steps

1. Share with someone that you have decided to follow Jesus Christ and have accepted Him as your Lord and Savior
2. Open up the bible and begin to jump into His Word. You can look up scriptures on a particular subject through the internet such as health, anxiety, fear, faith etc. for quick reverence
3. Talk to God daily. Its a conversation. Praying to God is your personal conversation. There is no wrong way. Like everything else, the way you prayer will grow. Praise the Lord by prayers of gratitude, by song, by dance, by art etc...
4. Find a physical and/or online church to join. Be intentional and submerge yourself. Do not stand on the outskirts. Come on in and get everything the Lord has for you. He loves you so much
5. Let us know that you decided to take leap of Faith by emailing to pamphletoflove@gmail.com I Chose Jesus.

There is always room to grow in Christ

To God be the Glory!

Thank you Lord for what you have put in my hands!

MissaJ

Messiah in sacrifice saved all Jesus

www.ingramcontent.com/pod-product-compliance
Lightning Source LLC
Chambersburg PA
CBHW042218050426
42453CB00001BA/12